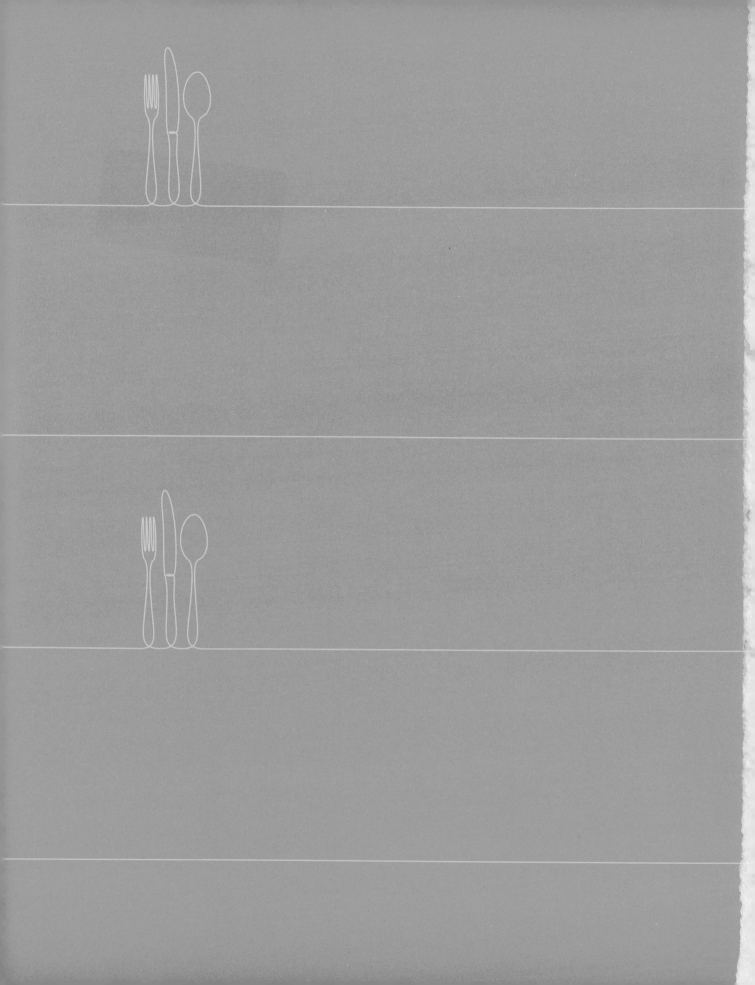

SiT & EAT

A Healthier Asian Cookbook

ISBN 978-981-5169-65-2 (hardback)
ISBN 978-981-5218-65-7 (epub)

Copyright © 2024 Singapore Institute of Technology

Published by Marshall Cavendish Cuisine
An imprint of Marshall Cavendish International

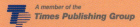
A member of the
Times Publishing Group

All rights reserved

No part of this publication may be reproduced, stored in a retrieval system or transmitted, in any form or by any means, electronic, mechanical, photocopying, recording or otherwise, without the prior permission of the copyright owner. Requests for permission should be addressed to the Publisher, Marshall Cavendish International (Asia) Private Limited, 1 New Industrial Road, Singapore 536196. E-mail: genref@sg.marshallcavendish.com   Website: www.marshallcavendish.com

Limits of Liability/Disclaimer of Warranty: The Author and Publisher of this book have used their best efforts in preparing this book. The parties make no representation or warranties with respect to the contents of this book and are not responsible for the outcome of any recipe in this book. While the parties have reviewed each recipe carefully, the reader may not always achieve the results desired due to variations in ingredients, cooking temperatures and individual cooking abilities. The parties shall in no event be liable for any loss of profit or any other commercial damage, including but not limited to special, incidental, consequential or other damages.

Other Marshall Cavendish Offices:
Marshall Cavendish Corporation, 800 Westchester Ave, Suite N-641, Rye Brook, NY 10573, USA • Marshall Cavendish International (Thailand) Co Ltd, 253 Asoke, 16th Floor, Sukhumvit 21 Road, Klongtoey Nua, Wattana, Bangkok 10110, Thailand • Marshall Cavendish (Malaysia) Sdn Bhd, Times Subang, Lot 46, Subang Hi-Tech Industrial Park, Batu Tiga, 40000 Shah Alam, Selangor Darul Ehsan, Malaysia

Marshall Cavendish is a registered trademark of Times Publishing Limited

National Library Board, Singapore Cataloguing in Publication Data

Name(s): Singapore Institute of Technology, author.
Title: SiT and eat : healthier Asian cooking / Singapore Institute of Technology.
Other Title(s): Singapore Institute of Technology and eat | Healthier Asian cookbook
Description: Singapore : Marshall Cavendish Cuisine, [2024]
Identifier(s): ISBN 978-981-5169-65-2 (hardback)
Subject(s): LCSH: Cooking, Asian. | Cooking (Natural foods) | Low-fat diet--Recipes. | Low-cholesterol diet--Recipes.
Classification: DDC 641.595--dc23

Printed in Singapore

Contents

Foreword 6
A Word from the Dietetics and Nutrition Team 8
Acknowledgements 11
About the Singapore Institute of Technology and its Dietetics & Nutrition Programme 12
Introduction 16

Main Meals

    Chickpea Tikka Masala with Naan **24**
vegan Eggplant Mapo Tofu with Brown Rice **26**
vegan Eggplant Unagi Donburi **28**
    Healthier Blue Pea Nasi Lemak with Achar and Chicken **30**
    Hidden Veggie Mac and Cheese **34**
    Homemade Fish Ball Noodle Soup **36**
vegan Miso Tofu Onigirazu **40**
    Oat Chicken Rendang with Brown Rice **44**
    Pork Bean Curd Roll **46**
    Pumpkin Chicken Congee **50**
    Savoury Pork Oats **52**
    Soy Milk Laksa **54**
    Tropical Omelette Wrap Sushi **56**
    Wholegrain Char Kway Teow **60**
    Wholemeal Carrot Cake **62**

Snacks & Desserts

    Air-Fried Pisang Goreng **68**
    Avocado Brownies **70**
vegan Baked Samosas **72**
vegan Bandung Kueh Salat **76**
    Chicken Vegetable Nuggets **78**
    Cocoa Tofu Mousse **80**
    Kueh Dadar **82**
    Low Fat Orh Nee **84**
vegan Pumpkin Chia Seed Ondeh Ondeh **86**
vegan Pumpkin Spread on Wholemeal Toast **90**
vegan Purple Bubur Chacha **92**
    Refreshing Dragon Fruit Yoghurt Bites **94**
    Watermelon Smoothie **96**
    Wholemeal Mantou with Sardine Potato Filling **98**
    Wholemeal Min Jiang Kueh **102**
    Yam Pumpkin Cake **104**
    Yoghurt Tiramisu **108**

Weights & Measures 112

Foreword

PROFESSOR CHUA KEE CHAING
SIT PRESIDENT

Food is one of Singapore's passions, deeply rooted in our society where diverse cultures and cuisines intermingle. In an ageing population like ours, a love for good food should come in tandem with a need to eat healthily. As individuals and communities place greater emphasis on their health and overall well-being, there is a growing demand for dietitians and nutrition experts, and their role has become more critical than ever.

At the Singapore Institute of Technology, our Bachelor of Science with Honours in Dietetics and Nutrition degree programme aims to address this growing demand. Upholding the principles of applied learning, we go beyond equipping Dietetics and Nutrition professionals with just the theoretical know-how. We also train our students to be able to step into the kitchen and cook delicious, healthy meals.

It is with great pride that I present this recipe book, a creation that reflects the collective dedication of our Dietetics and Nutrition students and faculty. Within these pages, you will discover 32 recipes that showcase the diverse tastes and preferences of the local Singaporean population. These recipes are meticulously designed to promote healthier eating, all while ensuring that the aroma, taste and textures of the dishes remain uncompromised.

I hope that this recipe book will be both a trusted guide in your kitchen as well as a fellow companion on your quest to create memorable, nutritious meals. Whether or not you are a seasoned cook or have just started your culinary journey, I am confident that this book will offer something appetising for you. I encourage you to experiment with these recipes, savour them and share them with your loved ones.

Embark on a journey of healthier eating today.

Happy cooking!

ASSOCIATE PROFESSOR TAN BHING LEET
CLUSTER DIRECTOR, HEALTH AND SOCIAL SCIENCES CLUSTER

I am delighted to share this remarkable recipe book, which is a culmination of the culinary and educational journey embarked upon by our Dietetics and Nutrition undergraduate students and academic staff here at SIT.

As part of the undergraduate programme's rigorous curriculum, kitchen labs are conducted to provide students with a unique opportunity to apply their theoretical knowledge to the practical realm of cooking. These labs have been conducted across various courses, such as "Human Nutrition", "Nutrition, Health and Disease", as well as "Medical Nutrition Therapy". In each of these courses, students are required to plan, design and cook menus based on case studies. The students are then evaluated not only on the appropriateness and suitability of their meals, but also on the crucial aspects of taste, texture, variety and creativity. This holistic evaluation process ensures that the recipes developed are not only nutritionally sound but also satisfying to the palate.

Healthier SG is a national initiative to encourage Singaporeans to take proactive steps to manage their health, prevent the onset of chronic diseases and tap on various resources to lead healthier lifestyles. With this recipe book, the Health and Social Sciences Cluster at SIT hopes to encourage Singaporeans to explore healthier alternatives to their diet and be convinced that healthy food can be delicious too. Whether you are seeking inspiration for something new to cook or want to take proactive steps to manage your health, we hope you will savour every moment and every bite.

Bon appétit!

ASSOCIATE PROFESSOR VERENA TAN
PROGRAMME LEADER, DIETETICS AND NUTRITION

The idea of putting together a collection of recipes from the Dietetics and Nutrition programme curriculum was first sparked in 2021 when I took over as the programme leader of the SIT Bachelor of Science with Honours in Dietetics and Nutrition degree programme, the first of its kind in Singapore.

In the world of food and nutrition, the kitchen is our laboratory. Through the kitchen labs, which are quintessentially part of the Dietetics curriculum, I witnessed how students cleverly modified familiar Asian recipes into healthier versions that taste just as good. This gave me the inspiration to collate their wonderful recipes into a book, a tribute to their creative dedication and hard work.

In these pages, you will find a diverse collection of recipes, from innovative, nutrient-packed breakfasts to wholesome, satisfying dinners and not to mention inventive twists on our local Asian desserts.

My favourite recipe in this book has to be the bandung kueh salat! It is a creative take on the classic Nyonya kueh we are familiar with. Visually, it's a stunner. Flavour-wise, it's a delight, as the subtle rose notes beautifully enhance the velvety bandung custard and chewy glutinous rice.

It is with great pride that I present to you, SiT & EAT, a collection of original and healthy interpretations of local dishes developed by our very own Dietetics and Nutrition students. So, let's get cooking and make every meal a delightful, nutritious and delicious experience!

Dig in!

Dr Claire Pettitt
Associate Professor

It has been such a pleasure to watch the students learn and grow through creating this recipe book. The recipes have been developed through passion and determination and a love of food. The skill of adapting classic recipes into healthier but still delicious alternatives is not easy, yet they have managed it with ease and created something which hopefully will become a staple in many households across Singapore!

Ms Ong Sik Yin
Senior Professional Officer

The students have impressed me with their creativity in coming up with the innovative healthy recipes. I am sure they will put their cooking skills to good use in inspiring everyone to cook and eat healthily!

Mr Gary Chiah
Senior Lecturer

The students' dedication to honing their therapeutic culinary skills is evident, and their creativity truly shines in the crafting of unique and delicious recipes. This cookbook is a testament to the students' hard work, passion for dietetics and love for cooking. Thank you for translating these ideas into reality. I would like to extend my best wishes and hope that those who pick up this book will greatly benefit from using it.

Acknowledgements

We would like to acknowledge the efforts and hard work of the following students who contributed to the recipe trials and photography:
Front row from left: Cheryl Leow Wenxuan, Brenna Tan Shi Ting, Baheera Binte Mohamed Ali.
Back row from left: Tan Jiahui, Ngm Yuxuan, Chong Jia En, Tay Yi Ting Jervin.

In addition, we would like to credit the SIT students in the Dietetics and Nutrition programme for sharing their innovative recipes, which were conceptualised as part of their kitchen lab activities.

About the Singapore Institute of Technology and its Dietetics & Nutrition Programme

The Singapore Institute of Technology (SIT) is Singapore's first university of applied learning. With a mission to maximise the potential of our students and to foster innovation with industry collaborations, SIT employs an integrated applied learning and research approach to contribute to economy and society.

Since its inception in 2009, SIT has been dedicated to applied learning, immersing students in authentic industry environments. This approach ensures that SIT graduates are well-prepared for real-world challenges, and ready to make meaningful contributions to their respective industries. The outcome of this practical approach is evident in this collection of recipes.

This recipe book is a collaborative effort between SIT and its Dietetics and Nutrition (DTN) students. It embodies the essence of applied learning ingrained in SIT's philosophy.

With a unique pedagogy that integrates clinical attachments into the curriculum, DTN students undergo clinical placements in various healthcare institutions and community settings. The hands-on cooking experiences in kitchen labs enable students to provide practical advice when designing suitable therapeutic diets for specific medical conditions. This cookbook showcases the innovative and creative spirit that defines our commitment to nurture skilled healthcare professionals prepared to impact society positively and meaningfully.

SIT currently encompasses six distributed campuses, with its main campus in SIT@Dover. The future campus will be nestled within the Punggol Digital District. This purpose-built campus is designed to provide practical, industry-focused education to equip students for life beyond academics. DTN students can look forward to a Dietetics Lab that comes fully equipped with a demo kitchen, consultation rooms and facilities for applied learning and research.

Envisioned as a vibrant community hub, the Punggol campus will not only cater to academic needs but also serve as a nucleus for collaborative learning and innovation. It symbolises the redefined landscape of higher education within a thriving community setting.

The Dietetics and Nutrition Team

Introduction

When the topic of healthier foods arises, what comes to mind? Many may envision salads or bland options like porridge. However, what if we were to share that even beloved local treats such as kueh salat, orh nee and the hawker favourite, laksa, can also be considered healthy options?

You may wonder who we are to assert the healthiness of these foods. We are a group of student dietitians from the Singapore Institute of Technology (SIT).

This cookbook marks the beginning of a series of cookbooks with the goal of reshaping negative perceptions surrounding healthy eating. After experimenting with numerous recipes in our kitchen labs and drawing from the experiences of the first four cohorts of student dietitians, we have curated the finest selections to present in the following pages. These recipes aren't just basic healthy eating tips. They are inventive approaches to crafting healthier versions of your favourite local classics within the comfort of your own home.

It's time to embark on a gastronomic adventure that tantalises your taste buds and propels you into a journey of healthy eating.

Let's get started!

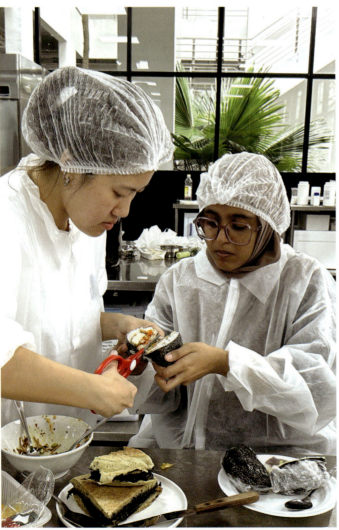

MAIN MEALS

Chickpea Tikka Masala with Naan

SERVES 3

This dish will warm you right up like a soothing embrace on a rainy day. The creamy, umami-packed masala is perfectly good on its own but downright heavenly when paired with fluffy naan. Rich in protein and high in fibre, this dish is absolutely divine for how little effort it takes to make it. What's more, it is perfect for meal prep too, as it freezes well, and can be reheated easily on the stove or microwave after work.

Ingredients

Naan
112.5 g self-raising flour
100 g Greek yoghurt

Chickpea Tikka Masala
246 g canned chickpeas
1 tbsp canola oil
3 g cumin seeds
3–4 cardamom pods
7–8 curry leaves
142 g brown/white onion, peeled and diced
½ tsp salt
1½ cloves garlic, peeled and minced
12 g ginger, peeled and minced
¾ tsp ground turmeric
3 g chilli powder
3 g garam masala
1 tbsp tomato paste
165 g tomatoes, diced
75 ml trim/light coconut milk

NUTRITION INFORMATION	Per Serve (310.9 g)	Per 100 g
Energy (kcal)	415	134
Protein (g)	14.3	4.6
Total fat (g)	15.8	5.1
Saturated fat (g)	6.6	2.11
Trans fat (g)	0	0
Cholesterol (mg)	3	1
Carbohydrate (g)	46.3	14.9
Dietary fibre (g)	13.0	4.2
Sodium (mg)	642.8	207

Method

Preparing the Naan

1. Combine flour and yoghurt in a bowl and knead until a dough is formed. Divide dough into 3 portions. Flatten and shape as desired.
2. Heat a frying pan over medium heat and cook naan without oil for about 5 minutes or until cooked through.

Preparing the Masala

3. Drain chickpeas. Rinse well and set aside.
4. Heat oil in a frying pan. Add cumin, cardamom and curry leaves and sauté for a minute.
5. Add onion and salt and continue to sauté until onions are translucent. Add garlic and ginger and sauté for another minute.
6. Add turmeric, chilli powder, garam masala, tomato paste and tomatoes and sauté for about 3 minutes.
7. Add chickpeas and cook for about a minute. Add some water if mixture is too dry. It should be slightly moist at this point.
8. Stir in coconut milk and cook for a few more minutes.
9. Remove from heat and garnish as desired. Enjoy with naan.

Tip: When shaping the dough, sprinkle some flour on the work surface and on your hands to prevent the dough from sticking.

Eggplant Mapo Tofu with Brown Rice *vegan*

SERVES 3

Mapo tofu is an iconic dish from Sichuan, China, that has become popular among many locals. A perfect medley of flavours with soft cubes of tofu and tender, melt-in-your-mouth eggplant, this dish is nothing short of perfect when paired with a warm bowl of rice. Treat yourself to this spicy, flavourful dish for a quick and gratifying weeknight dinner!

Ingredients

150 g uncooked mixed brown rice

Mapo Tofu

300 g eggplant
1 tsp canola oil
15 g ginger, peeled and minced
10 g garlic, peeled and minced
10 g chilli bean sauce
1 spring onion, chopped, white and green parts separated
1 tsp sesame oil
1 tsp miso
5 g raw sugar
7 ml reduced salt soy sauce
250 ml reduced salt liquid vegetable stock
350 g pressed tofu, cut into cubes
2 tsp white vinegar
150 ml water

NUTRITION INFORMATION

	Per Serve (680 g)	Per 100 g
Energy (kcal)	483	71
Protein (g)	16.4	2.4
Total fat (g)	9.6	1.4
Saturated fat (g)	1.4	0.2
Trans fat (g)	0	0
Cholesterol (mg)	0	0
Carbohydrate (g)	76.8	11.3
Dietary fibre (g)	9.4	1.4
Sodium (mg)	500	74

Method

1. Trim and discard ends of eggplant. Cut eggplant into wedges with skin on. Soak in water for 5 minutes. Drain before use.
2. Heat canola oil in a wok over medium heat. Add eggplant and pan-fry until golden brown.
3. Add ginger and garlic and stir-fry until golden brown.
4. Add chilli bean sauce, white part of spring onion and sesame oil. Stir-fry to mix.
5. Add miso, sugar, soy sauce and vegetable stock. Lower heat and let mixture simmer for at least 30 minutes or until sauce thickens.
6. In the meantime, cook rice in a rice cooker.
7. When sauce is of desired consistency, add pressed tofu and mix.
8. Add vinegar and water. Stir to mix and let sauce return to a simmer. Remove from heat.
9. Garnish with green part of spring onion. Serve with rice.

Eggplant Unagi Donburi *vegan*

SERVES 2

Although this dish is prepared using eggplant rather than unagi (eel), it is no less tantalising than the original dish as it features an equally scrumptious sauce. Donburi is a fantastic all-in-one rice bowl experience that is both simple to prepare and bursting with exquisite tastes.

Ingredients

160 g eggplant
2 tsp Japanese soy sauce
2 tbsp mirin
2 tbsp sake
2 tbsp sesame oil
2 tbsp water
Potato starch, as needed
2 tbsp canola oil
300 g cooked short-grain brown rice
A handful of chopped spring onion

NUTRITION INFORMATION

	Per Serve (353.6 g)	Per 100 g
Energy (kcal)	502	142
Protein (g)	6.9	2.0
Total fat (g)	19.3	5.5
Saturated fat (g)	2.9	0.8
Trans fat (g)	0.4	0.1
Cholesterol (mg)	0	0
Carbohydrate (g)	69.6	19.7
Dietary fibre (g)	2.7	0.8
Sodium (mg)	310	88

Method

1. Trim and discard ends of eggplant. Keep skin on or peel if desired. Slice eggplant lengthwise and steam for 10 minutes. Set aside to cool.
2. In the meantime, prepare sauce by combining soy sauce, mirin, sake, sesame oil and water. Set aside.
3. Lightly coat cooled steamed eggplant with potato starch.
4. Heat canola oil in a frying pan over medium heat. Place eggplant flat on pan and cook each side for 2–3 minutes or until nicely charred on both sides.
5. Brush sauce on one side of eggplant, then flip and coat other side. Repeat until eggplant is well glazed (about 2–3 times).
6. Serve atop rice. Garnish with spring onion.

Healthier Blue Pea Nasi Lemak with Achar and Chicken

SERVES 2

An undeniable hit at gatherings, this exquisite dish is bound to leave you craving for more. Featuring fragrant basmati rice infused with pandan and low fat evaporated milk, this nasi lemak pairs perfectly with pan-fried spiced chicken drumsticks and achar that offers a delightful balance of sweet and sour.

Ingredients

Blue Pea Rice
8 dried blue pea flowers
150 ml water
116 g uncooked Basmati rice
1 stalk lemongrass
1 pandan leaf
1.3-cm knob galangal, peeled and sliced
2 bay leaves
A pinch of salt
60 ml low fat evaporated milk

Achar (Makes 4 servings)
7 g fresh red chillies
3 g dried chillies
65 g Fuji apple
30 g pineapple
30 g tamarind paste
5 g ground turmeric
20 g garlic, peeled
40 g shallots, peeled
4 tsp canola oil
5 g white sugar
5 g balsamic vinegar
300 g cucumber, julienned
100 g carrot, peeled and julienned
100 g cabbage, cut into small pieces
15 g white sesame seeds

Chicken (Makes 4 servings)
8 shallots, peeled
4 cloves garlic, peeled
4 tsp ground turmeric
27 g ginger, peeled and chopped
Water, as needed
4 chicken drumsticks, skinned
1 1/3 stalks lemongrass, bruised
3 bay leaves
1 1/3 tsp salt
2/3 tsp ground white pepper
1 tbsp canola oil

NUTRITION INFORMATION

	Per Serve (705.8 g)	Per 100 g
Energy (kcal)	661	94
Protein (g)	36.6	5.2
Total fat (g)	29.4	4.2
Saturated fat (g)	6.1	0.9
Trans fat (g)	0	0
Cholesterol (mg)	248	35
Carbohydrate (g)	59.0	8.4
Dietary fibre (g)	8.1	1.2
Sodium (mg)	736	104

Method

Preparing the Blue Pea Rice

1. Steep dried blue pea flowers in 150 ml water overnight for intense blue colouring. Remove flowers before using.
2. Rinse and drain rice twice. Place in a rice cooker with blue pea water.
3. Bruise lemongrass, pandan leaf and galangal to release fragrance. Place on top of rice in rice cooker. Add bay leaves and salt.
4. Turn on rice cooker to cook rice for 30 minutes. When rice is done, fluff it up with chopsticks or a rice spatula.
5. Add evaporated milk and stir to coat rice evenly.
6. Close rice cooker and let rice cook for another 5 minutes. Fluff rice again. Repeat to fluff and let rice cook until evaporated milk is absorbed and rice is no longer wet.
7. Serve hot.

Preparing the Achar

8. Prepare spice paste. Place fresh chillies, dried chillies, apple, pineapple, tamarind paste, ground turmeric, garlic and shallots in a blender and process into a paste.
9. Heat canola oil in a wok over medium heat. Add spice paste and stir-fry until aromatic. Add sugar and balsamic vinegar and mix well.
10. Add cucumber, carrot and cabbage. Stir-fry for a few minutes until cabbage is cooked, then turn off the heat.
11. Sprinkle sesame seeds over, then dish out and set aside to cool. The achar can be served once it is cool. Alternatively, let it sit in the refrigerator overnight for better flavour development.

Preparing the Chicken

12. Prepare spice paste. Place shallots, garlic, ground turmeric and ginger in a blender with $1^{1}/_{3}$ tsp water. Process until fine and crumbly. Transfer to a mortar and pestle and pound into a smooth paste.
13. Place chicken in a small mixing bowl with 250 ml water, lemongrass, bay leaves, salt and pepper. Add spice paste and mix well.
14. Remove chicken and set aside to dry.
15. Heat canola oil in a pan over medium heat. Add chicken, turning it over with tongs every 1–2 minutes until it is golden brown all over.

Assembling the Nasi Lemak

16. Spoon some nasi lemak rice on a plate and serve with chicken and achar. You can also offer an optional side dish of hard-boiled eggs.

Hidden Veggie Mac and Cheese

SERVES 2

Looking to incorporate vegetables discreetly into your meals while retaining rich flavours? While mac and cheese may not be a familiar dish in Asian cuisine, it is a quintessential comfort food that appeals to both children and adults. We have taken a nutritious turn with this dish by integrating cauliflower, pumpkin and carrots into the creamy sauce, elevating the overall vitamin and mineral content.

Ingredients

- 40 g chicken breast meat
- 2 g coarsely ground black pepper
- Salt, as needed
- 110 g cauliflower
- 40 g skinned butternut squash
- 130 g carrot, peeled
- 12 ml olive oil
- 2 tsp garlic powder
- 2 tsp paprika
- 2 tsp mixed herbs
- 20 g garlic cloves, peeled
- 60 g macaroni
- 100 ml low fat milk
- 30 g mozzarella

NUTRITION INFORMATION

	Per Serve (277.8 g)	Per 100 g
Energy (kcal)	343	123
Protein (g)	19.0	6.8
Total fat (g)	11.9	4.3
Saturated fat (g)	3.6	1.3
Trans fat (g)	0.1	0
Cholesterol (mg)	23	8.2
Carbohydrate (g)	35.7	12.8
Dietary fibre (g)	8.7	3.1
Sodium (mg)	367	132

Method

1. Preheat oven to 200°C.
2. Marinate chicken with black pepper and a pinch of salt.
3. Dice chicken, cauliflower, butternut squash and carrot. Place on a baking tray and season with olive oil, garlic powder, paprika and mixed herbs. Scatter with garlic cloves.
4. Roast chicken and vegetables in the oven for 12 minutes or until chicken is cooked and vegetables are tender.
5. Keep oven heated.
6. Set aside chicken and about one-third of the cauliflower and carrot to be used as topping later.
7. Bring some water to the boil in a medium pot. Add a little salt and cook macaroni until al dente. Drain macaroni and measure out 80 ml of the water.
8. Prepare sauce. Place macaroni water and milk, with roasted carrot, cauliflower, butternut squash and garlic cloves in a blender. Process until smooth.
9. Place cooked macaroni in a casserole. Add blended sauce and reserved chicken, cauliflower and carrot.
10. Top with mozzarella and bake in the oven for 5 minutes or until cheese topping is browned.
11. Remove from oven. Garnish as desired and serve.

Homemade Fish Ball Noodle Soup

SERVES 4

The soup is prepared by simmering fish bones and tomatoes to create a fragrant foundation. The delightful, bouncy orbs of flavour are mild yet delectable, making them a versatile addition to various Southeast Asian dishes. The charm of these handcrafted fish balls lies in their irregular shape and texture, a telltale sign that they are made from real fish meat.

Ingredients

800 g wholemeal kway teow

400 g choy sum, cut into short lengths

20 g spring onion, chopped

Fish Balls

400 g yellowtail fish

¼ tsp salt

½ tsp ground white pepper

2 spring onions, chopped

1 fresh red chilli, chopped

Broth

4 medium tomatoes

4 small onions, peeled and quartered

4 red dates

40 g dried shrimp

2 litres water

½ tsp ground white pepper

2 tbsp rice bran oil

8 g ginger, peeled and sliced

12 g garlic, peeled and crushed

1 tbsp fish sauce

NUTRITION INFORMATION		
	Per Serve (1191.8 g)	Per 100 g
Energy (kcal)	596	50
Protein (g)	26.6	2.2
Total fat (g)	15.6	1.3
Saturated fat (g)	4.7	0.4
Trans fat (g)	0	0
Cholesterol (mg)	13	1
Carbohydrate (g)	83.1	7.0
Dietary fibre (g)	10.0	0.8
Sodium (mg)	781	65

Method

Preparing the Fish Balls

1. Debone fish. Cut meat into 2.5-cm chunks. Reserve bones for cooking broth.
2. Place fish meat in a blender and process into a smooth paste. Transfer to a medium bowl.
3. Add salt, pepper, spring onion and chilli and mix well.
4. Form and shape fish balls by grabbing a fistful of fish paste, then squeezing the paste between your thumb and index finger.

5. Place fish balls in a large bowl of warm water for them to firm up. When they are ready, the fish balls will float.
6. Bring a pot of water to a slow boil and drop the fish balls into the water. Boil for 5–10 minutes or until cooked through.

Preparing the Broth

7. Place all ingredients for broth, including reserved fish bones, in a pot. Bring to the boil, then lower heat and simmer for an hour or more for flavours to deepen.
8. When broth is ready, add kway teow, choy sum and spring onion to the pot to cook.
9. When choy sum is done, ladle broth with kway teow, choy sum and spring onion into serving bowls. Top with fish balls and serve.

"SiT down and slurp."

Miso Tofu Onigirazu *vegan*

SERVES 1

A fairly new creation, onigirazu cleverly melds the ingredients found in traditional onigiri with the convenience and form of a sandwich. Filled with the goodness of assorted vegetables, onigirazus retain their freshness for several hours after preparation, making them a practical and delicious option as a packed meal.

Ingredients

- 60 g uncooked Japanese rice
- 75 g firm tofu, cut into 2.5-cm thick slices, pat dry
- 2 tsp canola oil
- 60 g cabbage leaves, finely sliced
- 30 g carrot, peeled and cut into thin slivers
- 1 tsp sesame oil
- 2 nori sheets

Miso Marinade

- 1/3 tbsp white miso
- 1 tbsp water
- 1/3 clove garlic, peeled and minced
- 3 g ginger, peeled and minced

NUTRITION INFORMATION

	Per Serve (240.9 g)	Per 100 g
Energy (kcal)	339	141
Protein (g)	16.7	6.9
Total fat (g)	6.6	2.7
Saturated fat (g)	0.9	0.4
Trans fat (g)	0	0
Cholesterol (mg)	0	0
Carbohydrate (g)	50.8	21.1
Dietary fibre (g)	6.1	2.6
Sodium (mg)	318	132

Method

1. Soak rice for 30 minutes. Drain and cook using a 2:1 ratio of water to rice in the rice cooker or on the stove. Set aside to cool before using.
2. Combine all ingredients for miso marinade in a bowl. Add tofu and set aside for 30 minutes.
3. Heat 1 tsp oil in a pan over medium heat. Add cabbage and carrot, sesame oil and 1½ tbsp miso marinade. Cook until vegetables are softened. Dish out and set aside.
4. Heat remaining 1 tsp oil in a clean pan and pan-fry marinated tofu until golden brown. Set aside to cool.
5. Assemble onigirazu when ingredients are cool.
6. Place nori on a sheet of cling film. Press a thin layer of rice on nori, then top with 2 slices of tofu and some stir-fried carrot and cabbage. End with another layer of rice.
7. Fold opposite corners of nori over ingredients to form onigirazu. Wrap tightly with cling film to hold its shape. Slice onigirazu in half to serve.

Tip: An alternative method of presenting this dish is as a rice bowl. The nori can then be shredded and used as a topping.

Oat Chicken Rendang with Brown Rice

SERVES 4

Chicken rendang is a Malaysian-Indonesian delicacy. Despite its relatively concise ingredient list, the richness of flavours is truly astonishing. This lip-smacking dry curry presents chicken that's both succulent and flavourful, with intricate layers of taste enriched by the aromatic medley of exotic spices and coconut milk. The incorporation of oats serves a dual purpose: to strengthen the consistency of the sauce and to augment the dietary fibre content.

NUTRITION INFORMATION

	Per Serve (473.9 g)	Per 100 g
Energy (kcal)	604	128
Protein (g)	28.5	6.1
Total fat (g)	19.1	4.1
Saturated fat (g)	9.0	1.9
Trans fat (g)	0	0
Cholesterol (mg)	79	16.8
Carbohydrate (g)	75.4	16.0
Dietary fibre (g)	5.9	1.3
Sodium (mg)	273	58

Ingredients

100 g uncooked brown rice

Rempah
8 g dried chillies, soaked
50 g shallots, peeled
13 g garlic, peeled
13 g ginger, peeled
15 g galangal, peeled
2.5 g turmeric
18 g lemongrass

Rendang
30 g instant oats
2 g salt
2 g brown sugar
400 g boneless chicken thigh, cut into chunks
125 ml trim/light coconut milk
25 ml low fat milk
2 kaffir lime leaves

Method

1. Place oats in pan and dry-fry over low heat until lightly browned. Remove from heat and leave to cool for 5 minutes. Place in a blender and process until crumbly.
2. Prepare rempah. Place soaked dried chillies, shallots, garlic, ginger, galangal, turmeric and lemongrass in a blender and process into a paste. Pour into a pan.
3. Add salt and brown sugar. Bring to a simmer over medium heat.
4. Add chicken, coconut milk and milk. Continue to cook over medium heat for 25–30 minutes until chicken is tender and gravy is thick.
5. In the meantime, cook rice in a rice cooker.
6. When chicken is tender, add oat crumbs and lime leaves. Mix to incorporate and dish out.
7. Garnish rendang as desired. Serve hot with rice.

Pork Bean Curd Roll

SERVES 6

A delicious and popular dish that showcases the art of Chinese dim sum. Filled with a succulent and flavourful minced pork and vegetable stuffing, this steamed pork bean curd roll presents a savoury delight that can be eaten on its own or enjoyed alongside a serving of rice.

Ingredients

360 g minced pork
45 g red onion, peeled and minced
3 cloves garlic, peeled and minced
75 g carrot, peeled and minced
1½ spring onions, minced
1½ tbsp plain flour
A dash of ground white pepper
A pinch of salt
4½ eggs
Canola oil, as needed
4 sheets dried bean curd skin, each about 15 x 7-cm

NUTRITION INFORMATION	Per Serve (162.7 g)	Per 100 g
Energy (kcal)	230	142
Protein (g)	23.7	14.6
Total fat (g)	13.9	8.6
Saturated fat (g)	5.0	3.1
Trans fat (g)	0.1	0
Cholesterol (mg)	195	120
Carbohydrate (g)	2.1	1.3
Dietary fibre (g)	1.2	0.7
Sodium (mg)	127	78

Method

1. In a bowl, combine minced pork, onion, garlic, carrot and spring onions. Add flour, pepper and salt and mix well. Set aside.
2. In another bowl, whisk eggs.
3. Heat a little oil in a frying pan over medium heat. Add half the eggs and swirl to coat pan. Let egg cook into a thin omelette. Fold in half and set aside on a plate. Repeat to make another omelette.
4. Wipe bean curd sheets with a clean damp cloth to remove excess salt.
5. Place a bean curd sheet on a clean work surface. Spoon half the meat mixture on bean curd sheet and spread it out thinly. Top with an omelette. Place another bean curd sheet over omelette.
6. Fold two long sides of bean curd sheet in over omelette, then roll into a cylinder starting from the short end nearest you.
7. Repeat steps 5 and 6 with remaining ingredients.
8. Place rolls in a steamer and steam for 6–7 minutes or until meat is fully cooked.
9. Slice and serve hot. Enjoy!

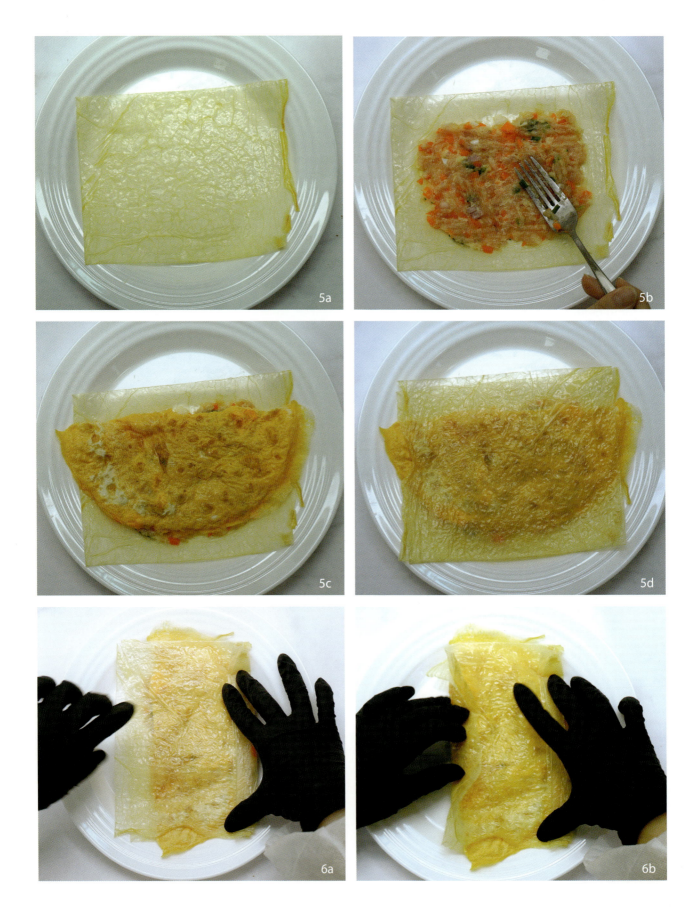

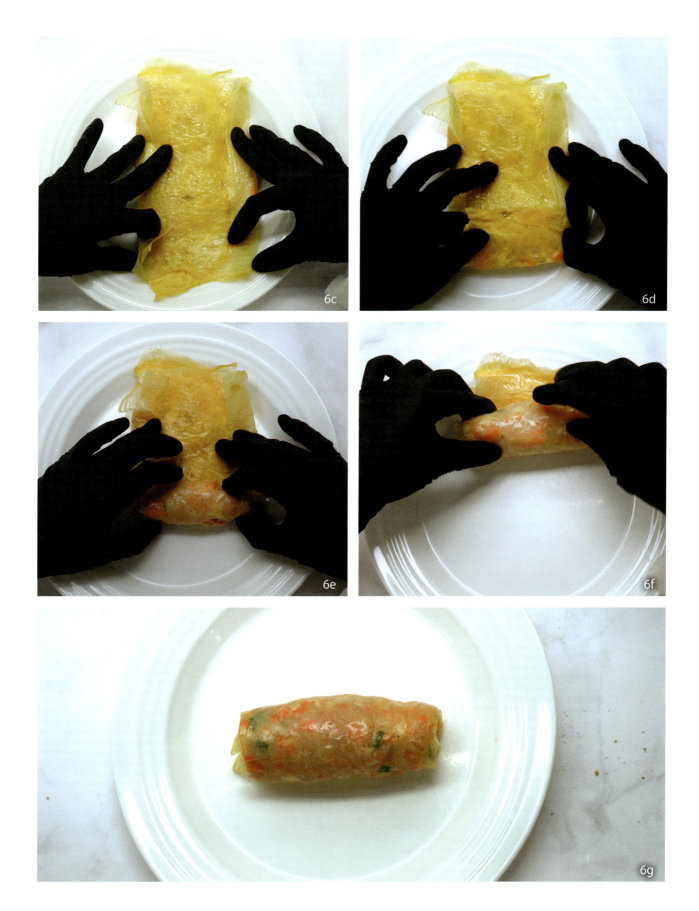

Pumpkin Chicken Congee

SERVES 1

Quick, comforting, and nourishing, this pumpkin congee requires only a handful of simple ingredients. The pumpkin adds natural sweetness, while silken tofu and spinach offer a comforting warmth. Ideal for serving up on chilly evenings, this congee is a fortifying and hearty meal option.

Ingredients

Congee
50 g uncooked white rice
Water, as needed
125 g pumpkin without skin, cut into cubes
50 g silken tofu, cut into cubes
175 g spinach, cut into short lengths

Chicken
90 g minced chicken
½ tsp light soy sauce
1¼ tsp dark soy sauce
1¼ sesame oil
½ tsp oyster sauce

Finishing
Sesame oil, to taste
1 spring onion, chopped

NUTRITION INFORMATION	Per Serve (510 g)	Per 100 g
Energy (kcal)	475	93
Protein (g)	31.9	6.3
Total fat (g)	14.9	2.9
Saturated fat (g)	3.2	0.6
Trans fat (g)	0.2	0
Cholesterol (mg)	71	14.0
Carbohydrate (g)	48.4	9.5
Dietary fibre (g)	8.2	1.6
Sodium (mg)	688	135

Method

1. Prepare congee base. Rinse rice and place in a rice cooker. Cook congee using a 1:1 ratio of water to rice.
2. Place minced chicken in a bowl. Add soy sauces, sesame oil and oyster sauce and mix well. Cover and refrigerate for 30 minutes.
3. Fill a pot with 500 ml water and bring to a boil. Add pumpkin and cooked rice. Lower the heat and simmer until pumpkin is soft.
4. Add marinated minced chicken and stir until congee is thick or of your preferred consistency.
5. Add tofu and spinach and cook for 2–3 minutes. Remove congee from heat.
6. Ladle congee into a bowl and drizzle with sesame oil. Top with spring onion and enjoy hot!

Savoury Pork Oats

SERVES 2

Oats, often associated with sweetness, shine equally in savoury fare like other grains. This flavourful pork oatmeal is a satisfying option anytime, offering versatility in toppings and add-ons based on what's available. Quick to assemble, this combination yields a robust flavour and delightful texture — a potential new go-to for effortless budget-friendly dining!

Ingredients

80 g minced pork
1 tsp ground white pepper
100 g silken tofu
500 ml water
40 g carrot, peeled and diced
3 g ginger, peeled and minced
3 g garlic, peeled and minced
34 g instant oats
1 tsp light soy sauce
1¼ tsp sesame oil
¼ tsp chicken seasoning powder
1½ tsp chopped spring onion

NUTRITION INFORMATION

	Per Serve (458.1 g)	Per 100 g
Energy (kcal)	308	67
Protein (g)	19.6	4.3
Total fat (g)	16	3.5
Saturated fat (g)	4.1	0.9
Trans fat (g)	0.2	0
Cholesterol (mg)	32	7
Carbohydrate (g)	19.0	4.1
Dietary fibre (g)	4.6	1.0
Sodium (mg)	212.7	46

Method

1. Place pork in a bowl and season with pepper.
2. Mash tofu and mix well with pork.
3. Bring water to a boil in a pot. Add carrot, ginger and garlic and continue to boil until carrot is soft.
4. Add minced pork mixture and cook for about a minute or until colour of pork changes and it is cooked.
5. Add oats and cook for 3–5 minutes or until mixture thickens slightly.
6. Season with soy sauce, sesame oil and chicken seasoning powder. Cook for another 2 minutes.
7. Ladle into a bowl and top with spring onion. Serve hot and enjoy!

Soy Milk Laksa

SERVES 2

Craving laksa but worried about its high fat content? Look no further! With this recipe, you can now indulge in your favourite dish that's been given a healthier twist without compromising on taste or flavour. As an alternative to coconut milk used in traditional laksa, soy milk helps bring this dish to a whole new level.

Ingredients

- 1 tbsp canola oil
- 4 stalks lemongrass, halved and bruised
- 5 kaffir lime leaves
- 400 ml sugar-free soy milk
- 320 g brown rice noodles
- 200 g long beans, trimmed and cut into short lengths
- 200 g enoki mushrooms, base trimmed
- 6 medium prawns, peeled

Laksa Paste

- 100 g dried shrimp
- 10 shallots, peeled
- 1 tsp grated ginger
- 1 tsp ground turmeric
- 5 g laksa leaves
- 4 stalks lemongrass
- 15 g dried chillies, soaked
- 85 ml canola oil

Method

1. Prepare laksa paste. Place all ingredients in a blender and process into a fine paste.
2. Heat a wok over medium heat. Add laksa paste and stir-fry for about 3 minutes. Set aside to cool. (See note.)
3. Heat canola oil in a pot over medium heat. Add 60 g laksa paste, lemongrass and kaffir lime leaves and stir-fry until fragrant.
4. Add soy milk and simmer for at least 20 minutes. If time permits, you may simmer the mixture for another 10 minutes to allow the flavours to develop further.
5. Add noodles, long beans, enoki mushrooms and prawns. Remove from heat when prawns are cooked.
6. Ladle into bowls and garnish as desired. Serve hot.

NUTRITION INFORMATION

	Per Serve (681.2 g)	Per 100 g
Energy (kcal)	614	90
Protein (g)	36.7	5.4
Total fat (g)	24.4	3.6
Saturated fat (g)	2.7	0.4
Trans fat (g)	0	0
Cholesterol (mg)	97	14
Carbohydrate (g)	64.4	9.5
Dietary fibre (g)	12.0	1.8
Sodium (mg)	505	74

Note: The laksa paste recipe yields about four times more paste than is required to make 2 servings of laksa. Store any excess paste in the refrigerator for future use.

Tropical Omelette Wrap Sushi

SERVES 2

Presented in an artistic arrangement on the plate, this sushi roll showcases a harmonious combination of elements. It starts with a layer of omelette and nori sheet, upon which a bed of tangy and sweet Japanese rice is delicately placed. This foundation is expertly rolled around a filling of creamy avocado and tenderly poached shrimp, with a satisfying crunch of carrot and cucumber matchsticks at its core. To infuse a burst of flavour, fresh mango slices are carefully added before the final rolling process.

Ingredients

Tamagoyaki Wrap

2 whole eggs
2 egg whites
1 tsp mirin
6 g sugar
2 tbsp canola oil

Maki

200 g uncooked Japanese rice
200 ml water
10 g kombu
4 tbsp Japanese sushi vinegar
6 medium prawns, peeled (and butterflied if desired)
100 g cucumber, cut into thin strips
100 g carrot, peeled and cut into thin strips
100 g avocado, skinned and cut into thin strips
100 g mango, peeled and cut into thin strips
2 nori sheets
Sushi soy sauce, to taste

NUTRITION INFORMATION

	Per Serve (508.3 g)	Per 100 g
Energy (kcal)	607	119
Protein (g)	28.3	5.6
Total fat (g)	30.1	5.9
Saturated fat (g)	3.9	0.8
Trans fat (g)	0	0
Cholesterol (mg)	231	45
Carbohydrate (g)	51.2	10.1
Dietary fibre (g)	8.1	1.6
Sodium (mg)	380	75

Tip: To know if a pan is hot, drop some egg mixture onto the pan as it heats. When you hear a sizzling sound, the pan is ready.

Method

Preparing the Tamagoyaki Wrap (Egg Sheets)

1. Combine whole eggs, egg whites, mirin and sugar in a bowl and mix well.
2. Heat a little oil in a medium frying pan over medium heat. Pour a thin layer of egg mixture into the pan, then quickly tilt pan so egg mixture coats the entire cooking surface.
3. Prick any air bubbles to release the air. When the bottom of the egg has set and the top is still soft, remove egg sheet and set aside. Repeat to make more egg sheets.
4. Leave egg sheets to cool before using.

Preparing the Maki

5. Reheat pan from cooking tamagoyaki. Using the residual oil, add prawns and stir-fry until just done. Set aside to cool.
6. Prepare rice. Rinse and drain rice at least 3 times until water is almost clear.
7. Place well-drained rice in a rice cooker with water. Place kombu on top of rice and set aside to soak for 20–30 minutes before turning the rice cooker on to cook rice.
8. When rice is cooked, discard kombu and transfer cooked rice to a large bowl. Drizzle sushi vinegar over rice. Using a rice paddle, gently 'slice' rice at a 45° angle to incorporate sushi vinegar and separate rice. Gently flip rice between 'slices'. Repeat this process until rice is cooled to room temperature. Set aside.

Assembling the Sushi Roll

9. Lay a sushi rolling mat on a clean work surface. Place a tamagoyaki sheet on the mat, followed by a sheet of nori.
10. Press a thin layer of rice on nori, leaving a 3 cm-wide border along edge furthest from you. Arrange strips of cucumber, carrot, avocado, mango and prawns in a line across centre of rice.
11. Using the rolling mat, roll ingredients away from you while keeping roll tight. The moisture from the rice will help it stick together.
12. Cut sushi roll into 6–8 pieces. Serve with sushi soy sauce for dipping.

Note: Since sushi vinegar would be added to the steamed rice, the rice is cooked on the firm side. As such, we use a 1:1 ratio of rice to water in this recipe.

Wholegrain Char Kway Teow

SERVES 2

Char kway teow holds a cherished place in the hearts of Southeast Asians. This beloved dish is a substantial medley, combining an array of meats, vegetables and satisfyingly chewy noodles. The technique employed here follows a 'one-pot' approach, where all components are expertly cooked together in a sizable frying pan. With its distinct wok hei essence, this rendition of char kway teow stands as an undeniable must-try dish!

Ingredients

4 medium prawns, peeled
A pinch of salt
A dash of ground white pepper
300 g choy sum
2 tsp canola oil
2 eggs, beaten
100 g bean sprouts
2 cloves garlic, peeled and minced
400 g wholegrain kway teow
50 g chives

Seasoning

2 tsp dark soy sauce
2 tsp light soy sauce
2 tsp sweet soy sauce
2 tsp oyster sauce
100 ml water

NUTRITION INFORMATION

	Per Serve (689.1 g)	Per 100 g
Energy (kcal)	558	81
Protein (g)	23.1	3.4
Total fat (g)	15.0	2.2
Saturated fat (g)	3.9	0.5
Trans fat (g)	0	0
Cholesterol (mg)	203	29
Carbohydrate (g)	79.1	11.5
Dietary fibre (g)	9.1	1.3
Sodium (mg)	1127	164

Method

1. Prepare seasoning by combining all ingredients. Set aside.
2. Marinate prawns with salt and pepper and set aside.
3. Remove fibrous stalk of choy sum and blanch in a pot of boiling water for 30 seconds. Drain and set aside.
4. Heat oil in a large non-stick pan over high heat. Add marinated prawns and cook for 4–5 minutes. Remove and set aside.
5. Add eggs to the same pan and scramble over medium heat.
6. Add bean sprouts and garlic and cook for about 1 minute.
7. Add blanched choy sum, kway teow, chives and cooked prawns. Mix well.
8. Add seasoning and gently toss mixture to mix evenly. Pause in between to allow kway teow to caramelise slightly.
9. Dish out and serve hot.

Wholemeal Carrot Cake

SERVES 4

A plate of charred carrot cake (chai tow kway) is akin to a warm hug full of nostalgia to many Singaporeans. The star of this Teochew dish is the soft, chewy cubes of steamed radish cake, stir-fried with garlic, eggs and preserved radish (chai poh) to create a delicious symphony of textures. Our version of the radish cake incorporates wholemeal flour to bump up its nutritional content while the homemade salted radish is a crunchy and healthier alternative to its store-bought counterpart. When everything is put together with just the right blend of seasonings and sauces, the resulting dish is nothing short of mouth-watering.

NUTRITION INFORMATION

	Per Serve (205.9 g)	Per 100 g
Energy (kcal)	265	128
Protein (g)	9.9	4.8
Total fat (g)	7.6	3.7
Saturated fat (g)	1.7	0.8
Trans fat (g)	0	0
Cholesterol (mg)	215	104
Carbohydrate (g)	36.7	17.8
Dietary fibre (g)	4.4	2.1
Sodium (mg)	685	333

Ingredients

Steamed Carrot Cake
- 68 g fine rice flour
- 68 g wholemeal flour
- 32 g tapioca flour
- 220 ml vegetable stock
- 200 ml water
- 200 g white radish, peeled and grated
- ¼ tsp olive oil
- 1⅓ tsp minced garlic

Salted Radish
- 100 g radish, peeled and diced
- 1 tsp salt

Fried Carrot Cake
- 4 tsp olive oil
- 2 tsp minced garlic
- 2 tsp sweet soy sauce
- 2 tsp chilli powder
- 4 drops fish sauce
- 4 eggs, beaten
- 2 tsp chopped spring onion

Method

Preparing the Salted Radish
1. Sprinkle radish with salt. Set aside for 30 minutes. Rinse off excess salt and set aside until needed.

Preparing the Steamed Carrot Cake
2. Whisk rice flour, wholemeal flour and tapioca flour with vegetable stock and water to achieve a thin batter. Set aside.
3. Boil a pot of water and add grated white radish. Cook for 6–8 minutes until radish is translucent. Drain and set aside.
4. Heat oil in a frying pan over medium heat. Add minced garlic and stir-fry until golden brown. Add rice flour mixture and stir continuously until mixture starts to thicken.
5. Add cooked grated radish and continue stirring. The batter should be thick. If it is too thin, continue cooking and stirring over low heat until mixture thickens.
6. Pour mixture into a baking tray. Cover and place in a steamer. Steam for 1 hour over medium-low heat until top is set. Set aside to cool before refrigerating overnight or for at least 2 hours.

Preparing the Fried Carrot Cake
7. Cut chilled carrot cake into small cubes.
8. Heat oil in a frying pan over medium heat. Add minced garlic and stir-fry until golden brown.
9. Add carrot cake and fry until slightly brown.
10. Add salted radish and continue frying for about 30 seconds. Add sweet soy sauce, chilli powder and fish sauce. Mix well.
11. Add beaten eggs, either pouring it over carrot cake or letting it cook at the side of the pan.
12. Stir everything together until uniform. Dish out and garnish with chopped spring onion. Offer sambal chilli on the side, if desired.

5b

5c

6a

6b

SNACKS & DESSERTS

Air-Fried Pisang Goreng

SERVES 2

As a local snack time staple, pisang goreng is a perfect marriage of sweet and savoury. In this healthy air-fried version, the batter is made with corn flour, egg whites and toasted wholemeal breadcrumbs to provide that perfect deep-fried pisang goreng texture. The balance of the crisp golden brown coating and sweet gooey banana is simply immaculate and will leave you craving for more! Satiate your cravings by snacking on these easy-to-make, air-fried, crispy banana fritters.

Ingredients

3 slices wholemeal bread
10 g corn flour
1 egg white, lightly beaten
2 ripe Cavendish bananas
Cooking oil spray

Method

1. Toast bread and blend until fine. Set aside in a small bowl.
2. Preheat air fryer to 180°C.
3. Place corn flour and egg white in separate bowls.
4. Peel bananas. Slice them across in half to get shorter pieces, then slice again lengthwise.
5. Coat bananas with a thin layer of corn flour, then dip into the egg white and coat with breadcrumbs.
6. Arrange bananas in a single layer in the air fryer. Air fry for 6 minutes, then flip the bananas over and air fry for another 6 minutes.
7. Serve hot and enjoy.

NUTRITION INFORMATION

	Per Serve (57.5 g)	Per 100 g
Energy (kcal)	81	141
Protein (g)	1.2	2.0
Total fat (g)	2.8	4.9
Saturated fat (g)	0.4	0.7
Trans fat (g)	0	0
Cholesterol (mg)	0	0
Carbohydrate (g)	11.8	20.4
Dietary fibre (g)	1.4	2.5
Sodium (mg)	20	35

Avocado Brownies

MAKES ONE 20-CM CAKE

Many interesting ingredients have been incorporated into brownies before but our personal favourite are avocados! Adding these not only improves the nutrition of the brownies but also their texture, giving them a fudgy and thick bite that is sure to satisfy your dessert cravings. Give our recipe a try the next time you feel like baking brownies, and we're sure you'll fall in love with this decadent and healthy sweet treat.

Ingredients

- 1 large avocado, peeled and pitted
- 2 large eggs at room temperature
- 73 g (⅓ cup) light brown sugar
- 85 g (¼ cup) pure maple syrup
- 3 tbsp unsalted butter at room temperature
- 1 tsp vanilla essence
- 43 g (½ cup) plus 2 tbsp unsweetened cocoa powder
- 63 g (½ cup) blanched almond flour
- 1 tsp instant coffee powder
- 1 tsp baking soda
- ½ tsp kosher salt
- 42.5 g (¼ cup) chocolate chips

NUTRITION INFORMATION

	Per Serve (20.7 g)	Per 100 g
Energy (kcal)	78	380
Protein (g)	1.6	7.9
Total fat (g)	3.5	16.9
Saturated fat (g)	0.6	3.0
Trans fat (g)	0	0
Cholesterol (mg)	1	4
Carbohydrate (g)	9.9	47.7
Dietary fibre (g)	1.5	7.4
Sodium (mg)	142	688

Method

1. Preheat oven to 180°C.
2. Line a 20-cm square baking tray with parchment paper, leaving an overhang on two sides. Lightly coat surface of parchment paper with oil/non-stick spray and set aside.
3. In a food processor, combine all ingredients except for chocolate chips. Blend until smooth with no lumps, stopping to scrape down the sides of the food processor bowl from time to time.
4. Add half the chocolate chips and pulse several times to roughly incorporate.
5. Pour batter into prepared tray. Smoothen top.
6. Sprinkle remaining chocolate chips on top.
7. Bake for 25–30 minutes until top is set and a toothpick inserted into the centre of cake comes out mostly clean with just a few moist crumbs.
8. Place tray on a wire cooling rack and cool for 30 minutes. Using parchment paper handles, lift cake from tray and place on rack to cool completely.
9. Slice into 16 pieces and serve.

Baked Samosas *vegan*

MAKES 15

Samosas tend to be quite greasy and high in fat due to being deep-fried in oil. For a health-conscious take on this well-loved snack, baking is the way to go! While making samosas may look a little daunting at first, they are actually quite simple to make and are a great way to add more fibre into your diet. Flavourful curry-seasoned vegetables wrapped within a crisp, flaky skin. Honestly, what more could you ask for?

Ingredients

120 g cauliflower
50 g potato, peeled
50 g carrot, peeled
50 g green peas
7 g curry powder
15 spring roll wrappers
3 g canola oil for brushing

NUTRITION INFORMATION

	Per Serve (66 g)	Per 100 g
Energy (kcal)	63	95
Protein (g)	2.2	3.4
Total fat (g)	1.5	2.3
Saturated fat (g)	0.5	0.7
Trans fat (g)	0	0
Cholesterol (mg)	0	0
Carbohydrate (g)	9.3	14.1
Dietary fibre (g)	1.7	2.5
Sodium (mg)	179	271

Method

Preparing the Samosa Filling

1. Heat a pot of water over high heat.
2. In the meantime, cut cauliflower, potato and carrot into small pieces. Place in separate bowls.
3. Once water is boiling, lower heat to medium. Add potato and cook until fork-tender. Remove to a bowl and repeat for carrot, cauliflower and peas.
4. Add curry powder and a pinch of salt to cooked vegetables, then mash with a fork or potato masher.

(Recipe continues)

Making the Samosa

5. Preheat oven to 200°C. Line a sheet pan with baking paper.
6. Place a spring roll wrapper on a clean cutting board or work surface.
7. Fold the bottom right corner of the wrapper up to meet the upper left hand corner to form a triangle.
8. Fold the upper right hand corner down to meet the centre folding line.
9. Wet the straight edge with some water, then fold it upwards to start forming the pocket of the samosa.
10. Take the furthest corner on the right and fold it towards the base of the pocket.
11. Pick up the wrapper and open it up to form a cone. Spoon about 1½ tbsp filling into the cone and spread it out evenly. (The amount of filling can be adjusted according to the size of the spring roll wrapper used.)
12. Wet the edges of the cone with some water, then start sealing the cone by folding down the small flaps, and ending with the big flap.
13. Apply more water to seal the wrapper if needed.
14. Brush samosa with some oil and place on lined sheet pan.
15. Repeat steps 2–10 to make more samosas. Keep samosas about 4 cm apart.
16. Bake samosas for 20 minutes or until golden brown on top. Turn samosas over and bake for another 5–8 minutes to brown the other side.
17. Transfer to a serving plate and serve.

Bandung Kueh Salat *vegan*

SERVES 5

A bed of chewy glutinous rice topped with sweet, fragrant coconut custard, infused with subtle floral notes. This rendition of the classic Nyonya kueh incorporates the familiar flavours of bandung through the use of rose petals, giving the kueh a pretty pink hue. Despite the use of trimmed coconut milk, the custard still maintains the richness and fragrance that kueh salat is known for.

Ingredients

Rice Layer
- 150 g uncooked glutinous rice
- 2 pandan leaves, cleaned and knotted
- 50 ml trim/light coconut milk
- 50 ml water
- ¼ tsp salt

Bandung Custard
- 15 g rose petals
- 60 ml hot water
- 40 g plain flour
- 15 g cornstarch
- 60 g monk fruit sweetener
- 150 ml trim/light coconut milk
- 1 drop red food colouring

NUTRITION INFORMATION

	Per Serve (120.5 g)	Per 100 g
Energy (kcal)	199	165
Protein (g)	2.1	1.7
Total fat (g)	9.9	8.2
Saturated fat (g)	8.6	7.2
Trans fat (g)	0	0
Cholesterol (mg)	0	0
Carbohydrate (g)	24.0	19.9
Dietary fibre (g)	0.7	0.5
Sodium (mg)	126	105

Tip: To get a stronger rose flavour, use a spoon to press down on the rose petals while they are soaking.

Method

Preparing the Rice Layer
1. Soak glutinous rice in water for at least 1 hour.
2. Drain rice and place in a steamer with pandan leaves, coconut milk, water and salt. Steam over high heat for 25 minutes.
3. Remove and discard pandan leaves.
4. Fluff steamed rice using a fork or chopsticks and set aside to cool.
5. Transfer cooled rice to a greased 10 x 6-cm baking tray. Using the flat side of a spatula, gently press rice down to pack it and form a smooth surface.

Preparing the Custard
6. Soak rose petals in hot water for 10 minutes or until petals are a very light shade of pink/white. Remove and discard rose petals. Set rose water aside.
7. Combine rest of ingredients in a mixing bowl using a whisk. Add rose water and mix well.
8. Pass mixture through a sieve to remove any lumps, then pour over packed rice in baking tray.
9. Gently tap tray to remove any air bubbles.

Steaming the Kueh
10. Steam mixture for 25–30 minutes over medium heat until custard is completely cooked through.
11. Remove kueh from steamer and allow to cool before unmoulding. Slice to serve.

SiT & EAT Snacks & Desserts

Chicken Vegetable Nuggets

SERVES 5

A healthy spin on a classic bite-sized snack with the addition of vegetables. This is as simple as it gets — just combine the ingredients, shape the mixture as desired and pop them into an air fryer! You could also make a large batch, then freeze and air-fry them whenever you need to rustle up a quick snack or a last-minute side dish.

Ingredients

75 g ginger

75 g white onion

140 g carrot

140 g broccoli

225 g minced chicken

A dash of ground white pepper

30 g sesame oil

25 g cornflour

75 g cornflakes

Method

1. Peel ginger, onion and carrot, then mince as finely as possible.
2. Mince broccoli as finely as possible.
3. Add minced vegetables to minced chicken and mix well. Season with pepper, sesame oil and cornflour.
4. Place cornflakes in a clean plastic bag and crush as finely as possible.
5. Shape minced chicken mixture into nuggets and coat with crushed cornflakes.
6. Air-fry or bake vegetable nuggets at 180°C for about 8 minutes on each side.

NUTRITION INFORMATION	Per Serve (163.7 g)	Per 100 g
Energy (kcal)	294	180
Protein (g)	13.9	8.5
Total fat (g)	14.4	8.8
Saturated fat (g)	2.6	1.6
Trans fat (g)	0.2	0.1
Cholesterol (mg)	36	22
Carbohydrate (g)	23.2	14.2
Dietary fibre (g)	8.4	5.1
Sodium (mg)	152	93

Cocoa Tofu Mousse

SERVES 4

This chocolate delight may look like a downright sinful dessert but it is actually chock-full of protein, all thanks to the inclusion of a not-so-secret ingredient — silken tofu! Aside from giving this mousse its smooth and creamy texture, tofu is also a fantastic source of plant protein that helps keep you satisfied for longer. This high protein dessert is simple to make and would no doubt satisfy your sweet cravings.

Ingredients

300 g silken tofu
30 g creamy peanut butter
2 tsp vanilla essence
3 tbsp cocoa powder
40 g honey

Method

1. Place all the ingredients in a blender and process until a smooth consistency is achieved.
2. Transfer to individual serving cups or bowls and refrigerate for at least 4 hours to chill.
3. Serve with your favourite toppings!

NUTRITION INFORMATION	Per Serve (102.5 g)	Per 100 g
Energy (kcal)	153	149
Protein (g)	7.6	7.4
Total fat (g)	8.1	7.9
Saturated fat (g)	1.7	1.7
Trans fat (g)	0	0
Cholesterol (mg)	0	0
Carbohydrate (g)	11.0	10.7
Dietary fibre (g)	3.9	3.8
Sodium (mg)	11	11

Kueh Dadar

SERVES 12

These vibrantly coloured, fragrant pandan crepes stuffed with a sweet coconut filling have been given a healthy twist. Using oat flour, each roll provides not only a burst of sweetness for a perfect midday snack, but also fibre for longer lasting satisfaction. But that's not all. With a partial substitution of the palm sugar with an all-natural monk fruit sweetener, this snack is also lower in sugar content and calories.

NUTRITION INFORMATION	Per Serve (76.6 g)	Per 100 g
Energy (kcal)	306	400
Protein (g)	4.1	5.3
Total fat (g)	19.2	25.1
Saturated fat (g)	14.7	19.2
Trans fat (g)	0	0
Cholesterol (mg)	43	56.1
Carbohydrate (g)	27.0	35.2
Dietary fibre (g)	5.2	6.7
Sodium (mg)	97	127

Ingredients

Pandan Crepes
85 g oats
5–6 pandan leaves, cleaned
120 ml water
3 tbsp tapioca starch
125 ml trim/light coconut milk
2 eggs
½ tsp vanilla essence
Olive/coconut oil spray

Filling
75 g desiccated coconut
40 g palm sugar (gula Melaka)
20 g monk fruit sweetener
60 ml water
1 pandan leaf, cleaned and knotted

Method

Preparing the Crepes
1. Blend oats until it resembles flour. Set aside.
2. Roughly cut pandan leaves and blend with water. Strain mixture and pour pandan liquid back into blender.
3. Add oat flour, tapioca starch, coconut milk, eggs and vanilla into the blender and process until batter is smooth.
4. Heat a small non-stick pan over medium heat. Once hot, spray with some olive/coconut oil.
5. Add ¼ cup batter and swirl quickly to form a crepe. Allow to cook for 4–5 minutes. While the crepe is cooking, use a spatula to go round under the edges of the crepe to make sure the crepe isn't sticking to the pan.
6. Flip the crepe and cook for another 4–5 minutes before removing to a plate.
7. Repeat steps 5 and 6 to make more crepes.

Preparing the Filling
8. Divide desiccated coconut into 2 equal portions.
9. Heat a frying pan over medium heat. Add a portion of desiccated coconut and toast until it turns a deep golden brown colour. Remove and set aside to cool.
10. To the same frying pan, add palm sugar, sweetener, water and pandan leaf. Heat until sugar is completely dissolved.
11. Stir in second portion of desiccated coconut and mix well. Remove and set aside to cool.
12. When cool, add toasted desiccated coconut and mix well.

Assembling the Kueh Dadar
13. Place 1 tbsp filling onto the centre of a crepe. Fold the left and right sides of the crepe over the filling, then roll into a log. Enjoy!

Low Fat Orh Nee

SERVES 1

An old-school Teochew dessert with decades of history and nostalgia. Lighter yet equally satisfying, this classic, warm, smooth and comforting orh nee is lower in saturated fat than regular orh nee.

Ingredients

100 g taro, peeled and cut into small chunks
5 g honey
8.5 ml trim/light coconut milk
40 ml oat milk

Method

1. Place the taro chunks in a steamer and cook for 15–20 minutes until soft.
2. Mash taro with a fork until minimal lumps are left.
3. Pass mashed taro through a sieve to remove any lumps.
4. Mix in honey, coconut milk and milk. Stir until a smooth paste is formed.
5. Serve warm, topped with gingko nuts and pumpkin paste, if desired.

NUTRITION INFORMATION

	Per Serve (115.1 g)	Per 100 g
Energy (kcal)	127	110
Protein (g)	2.0	1.8
Total fat (g)	2.3	2.0
Saturated fat (g)	1.4	1.3
Trans fat (g)	0	0
Cholesterol (mg)	0	0
Carbohydrate (g)	22.6	19.7
Dietary fibre (g)	3.0	2.6
Sodium (mg)	24	21

Pumpkin Chia Seed Ondeh Ondeh *vegan*

SERVES 4

Ondeh ondeh is a local sweet treat with a delightfully soft and chewy texture. The burst-in-your-mouth sweetness is what makes this such an irresistible treat! Our version of the chewy coconutty treat is bright yellow in colour, thanks to the use of pumpkin which, along with chia seeds, provides added fibre. This healthier version has truly been designed for you to enjoy without compromising on the taste.

Ingredients

60 g pumpkin without skin, cut into chunks
300 ml water
2 pandan leaves, cleaned and knotted
85 g glutinous rice flour
7.5 g chia seeds
50 g palm sugar (gula Melaka), chopped
60 g desiccated coconut

Method

1. Steam pumpkin for 10 minutes until soft, then mash with a fork.
2. Place 300 ml water and pandan leaves in a pot and boil for 5–10 minutes. Remove pandan leaves and set aside to cool.
3. In a large bowl, mix glutinous rice flour with mashed pumpkin. Gradually add 80 ml pandan water and knead to form a smooth dough. If dough is too dry, add a little more pandan water. If dough is too wet, add a little more flour.
4. Take about 10 g dough and roll into a ball. Flatten it slightly and top with ½ tsp chia seeds and some palm sugar. Bring edges of dough up to enclose filling. Pinch to seal, then roll into a smooth ball. Repeat with the rest of the ingredients.
5. Bring a pot of water to a boil and gently lower balls into the boiling water to cook. When they start to float, leave to cook for another 2–3 minutes before removing with a slotted spoon.
6. Coat balls with desiccated coconut and serve warm.

NUTRITION INFORMATION

	Per Serve (78.3 g)	Per 100 g
Energy (kcal)	179	228
Protein (g)	3.2	4.1
Total fat (g)	1.3	1.7
Saturated fat (g)	0.4	0.5
Trans fat (g)	0	0
Cholesterol (mg)	0	0
Carbohydrate (g)	38.2	48.8
Dietary fibre (g)	2.7	3.4
Sodium (mg)	15	19

SiT & EAT Snacks & Desserts

4f

4g

5

6

89

Pumpkin Spread on Wholemeal Toast *vegan*

SERVES 2

Toast is arguably quite boring on its own. However, once it is dressed up with a dollop of sweet, sticky Nyonya kaya, it is nothing short of irresistible. Our smooth and creamy plant-based pandan-pumpkin spread is reminiscent of Nyonya kaya. Made using pumpkin, oat milk, pandan and monk fruit sweetener, this spread is a tasty, healthy and vegan rendition of the classic beloved spread.

Ingredients

- 120 g pumpkin without skin, cut into chunks
- 50 ml oat milk
- 20 g monk fruit sweetener
- 4 pandan leaves, cleaned and knotted
- 4 slices wholemeal bread

Method

1. Steam pumpkin for 15–20 minutes until soft.
2. Place steamed pumpkin into a blender with oat milk and monk fruit sweetener and blend until smooth.
3. Pour mixture into a saucepan. Add pandan leaves and stir over medium heat until sweetener is dissolved.
4. Remove mixture from heat and transfer to a clean airtight jar. If stored correctly, this spread will keep refrigerated for up to 3 months.
5. Toast bread and top with pumpkin spread. Enjoy!

NUTRITION INFORMATION

	Per Serve (151.2 g)	Per 100 g
Energy (kcal)	195	129
Protein (g)	8.3	5.5
Total fat (g)	2.0	1.3
Saturated fat (g)	0.3	0.2
Trans fat (g)	0	0
Cholesterol (mg)	0	0
Carbohydrate (g)	31.9	21.1
Dietary fibre (g)	6.7	4.4
Sodium (mg)	267	177

Purple Bubur Chacha *vegan*

SERVES 5

Bubur chacha is a popular dessert in Singapore known for its beautiful mix of colours. It consists of chewy sago, and steamed taro and sweet potato cubes in fragrant pandan leaf-infused coconut milk. Enjoy at any time of the day!

Ingredients

100 g taro, peeled and cut into cubes

100 g purple sweet potato, peeled and cut into cubes

Water, as needed

40 g sago

30 g sugar

2–3 pandan leaves, cleaned and knotted

110 ml trim/light coconut milk

110 ml almond/hazelnut milk

Method

1. Steam taro and sweet potato cubes for 20 minutes. Set aside.
2. Bring a pot of water to the boil. Add sago and cook until translucent, stirring occasionally so that sago does not stick to the bottom of the pot.
3. Strain cooked sago and place in a pot of cold water to prevent them from sticking together.
4. In another pot, add sugar, 260 ml water and pandan leaves. Bring to the boil over medium heat.
5. Add coconut milk and milk and return to the boil.
6. Add steamed taro and sweet potato cubes and sago. Lower heat and let mixture simmer for 10 minutes or until desired texture is reached.
7. Serve hot.

NUTRITION INFORMATION	Per Serve (99.2 g)	Per 100 g
Energy (kcal)	157	158
Protein (g)	1.5	1.5
Total fat (g)	5.7	5.8
Saturated fat (g)	4.7	4.7
Trans fat (g)	0	0
Cholesterol (mg)	0	0
Carbohydrate (g)	24.1	24.3
Dietary fibre (g)	1.4	1.4
Sodium (mg)	85	85

Refreshing Dragon Fruit Yoghurt Bites

SERVES 6

This simple yet delicious dessert celebrates the vibrant dragon fruit. With a yummy yoghurt base and the addition of chia seeds and walnuts, this tasty frozen dessert is not only healthy, it also provides a refreshing respite from the sweltering Singapore heat.

Ingredients

140 g natural yoghurt
130 g red dragon fruit without skin
15 g walnuts, crushed
2.5 g chia seeds

Method

1. Line a 6-hole muffin tin with paper cases or use silicone moulds.
2. Pour yoghurt evenly into each mould and place in the freezer for an hour or until yoghurt is frozen.
3. In the meantime, blend dragon fruit until smooth.
4. Pour dragon fruit purée evenly over frozen yoghurt layer and top with crushed walnuts and chia seeds.
5. Return to the freezer for at least another hour or until dragon fruit layer is frozen. Serve.

NUTRITION INFORMATION

	Per Serve (47.9 g)	Per 100 g
Energy (kcal)	46	95
Protein (g)	2.2	4.6
Total fat (g)	2.0	4.2
Saturated fat (g)	0.2	0.4
Trans fat (g)	0	0
Cholesterol (mg)	1	2
Carbohydrate (g)	4.1	8.5
Dietary fibre (g)	0.7	1.5
Sodium (mg)	20	42

Watermelon Smoothie

SERVES 4

Let's be honest about it. The motivation to do anything other than the bare minimum melts away when the blistering heat of the tropical sun hits. Quench your thirst and refresh yourself with this perfectly creamy and naturally sweet luscious watermelon smoothie.

Ingredients

260 g watermelon without skin, chopped
800 ml low fat milk
Ice cubes, as desired

Method

1. Place watermelon and milk in a blender and process until smooth and creamy.
2. Pour into glasses filled with ice and serve.

NUTRITION INFORMATION	Per Serve (237 g)	Per 100 g
Energy (kcal)	119	44
Protein (g)	8.1	3.0
Total fat (g)	2.7	1.0
Saturated fat (g)	1.8	0.6
Trans fat (g)	0.1	0
Cholesterol (mg)	11	4
Carbohydrate (g)	15.4	5.7
Dietary fibre (g)	0.3	0.1
Sodium (mg)	88	32

Wholemeal Mantou with Sardine Potato Filling

SERVES 8

Discover how to craft mantou that are irresistibly soft and generously packed with a savoury, spicy and aromatic sardine potato filling. This delectable treat will satisfy your taste buds while remaining kind to your wallet. The filling, made using canned sardines, helps simplify the cooking process. With the use of fragrant spices and seasonings, you're well on your way to a culinary delight that's bound to impress.

Ingredients

Dough

160 g superfine wholemeal flour

80 g cake flour + extra for dusting

3.2 g instant dry yeast

16 g sugar

A pinch of salt

1 tbsp canola oil

200 g low fat milk, warmed

Filling

160 g potato, peeled

Cooking oil spray

1 yellow onion, peeled and chopped

3½ tsp chopped garlic

A pinch of salt

2 tbsp fish curry powder

1¾ tsp chilli powder

117 g canned sardines in tomato sauce

1 spring onion, chopped

NUTRITION INFORMATION		
	Per Serve (111.5 g)	Per 100 g
Energy (kcal)	190	170
Protein (g)	8.2	7.3
Total fat (g)	4.9	4.4
Saturated fat (g)	1.0	0.9
Trans fat (g)	0	0
Cholesterol (mg)	14	13
Carbohydrate (g)	26.0	23.3
Dietary fibre (g)	4.8	4.3
Sodium (mg)	199	179

Method

Preparing the Mantou

1. Combine all ingredients and knead for about 15 minutes until it forms a smooth dough. Let dough rest for about 15 minutes.
2. Knead dough for another 15 minutes until it forms a smooth ball shape. Divide dough into 8 equal portions. Knead each portion into a ball. Then, using a rolling pin, roll each ball into an oval.
3. Cover dough and set aside for 45 minutes.
4. Place dough in a lined steamer and steam for 15 minutes. Set aside to cool.

Preparing the Filling

5. Boil a pot of water and cook potato until soft. Lightly mash with a fork.
6. Heat a pan over medium heat and spray with oil. Add onion and garlic and cook until onion is soft and translucent. Season with salt, fish curry powder and chilli powder.
7. Add sardines with tomato sauce and mix well. Using a spatula, mash sardines into small pieces.
8. Add mashed potato and mix well. Cook until mixture is thick and moist, but with no excess liquid. Dish out.

Assembling the Mantou

9. Slice mantou, but do not cut all the way through. Stuff generously with filling. Garnish with spring onion and serve.

Wholemeal Min Jiang Kueh

SERVES 12

Min jiang kueh is a traditional pancake that is widely enjoyed in Singapore as an on-the-go breakfast or snack. Soft, fluffy and quite frankly, a sweet tooth's dream, this healthier version of the beloved pancake is made using wholemeal flour and soy milk as its main ingredients. Fill your min jiang kueh generously with our simple yet delectable honey-black sesame paste and enjoy to your heart's content!

Ingredients

Pancakes
- 150 g wholemeal flour
- 150 g plain flour
- 120 g sugar
- 1 tsp baking soda
- 1 tsp instant dry yeast
- A pinch of salt
- 2 large eggs
- 500 ml soy milk
- Cooking oil spray

Black Sesame Paste
- 2 cups toasted black sesame seeds
- 4 tbsp honey

NUTRITION INFORMATION

	Per Serve (112.3 g)	Per 100 g
Energy (kcal)	285	254
Protein (g)	10.0	8.9
Total fat (g)	15.1	13.4
Saturated fat (g)	2.0	1.8
Trans fat (g)	0.3	0.3
Cholesterol (mg)	42	37
Carbohydrate (g)	25.5	22.7
Dietary fibre (g)	4.4	3.4
Sodium (mg)	163	145

Method

Preparing the Black Sesame Paste
1. Place toasted black sesame seeds and honey in a blender and process until a thick and smooth paste is formed. Store in a clean jar. If stored correctly, this paste will keep refrigerated for up to a month and frozen for up to 6 months.

Preparing the Pancakes
2. In a large bowl, place wholemeal flour, plain flour, sugar, baking soda, yeast and a pinch of salt. Mix well.
3. In another bowl, beat eggs and add soy milk. Gradually add to dry mixture while whisking to ensure there are no clumps.
4. Cover batter with a damp tea towel and let sit for an hour.
5. Heat a 26-cm round non-stick pan over low heat and spray lightly with oil. Spoon 3 ladles of batter into pan and swirl to coat pan evenly.
6. Allow to cook uncovered for 30 seconds, then cover pan with a lid and cook for 2 minutes. The bottom of the pancake should be a light golden brown while the surface is soft and springy.
7. Once done, transfer pancake to a plate or cutting board and allow to cool.
8. Repeat steps 4–6 to make more pancakes.

Assembling the Min Jiang Kueh
9. Spread some sesame paste on each pancake, then fold in half and cut into wedges.
10. Enjoy with your favourite cup of tea!

Yam Pumpkin Cake

SERVES 6

With this twist of the traditional yam cake, we promise to send you on a gastronomic adventure. Unlike the classic version, this recipe takes advantage of the sweetness from the pumpkin to balance out the savoury flavours in the yam cake. Overall, our version achieves the same level of satisfaction with less salt and oil, making this delicacy healthier.

Ingredients

18 g dried shiitake mushrooms
40 g dried shrimps
Water, as needed (see Tip)
20 g shallots, peeled
125 g pumpkin
125 g yam
200 g rice flour
40 g tapioca starch
2 tbsp canola oil

Seasoning
1 tsp ground white pepper
¼ tsp five spice powder
6 g oyster sauce
2 tsp light soy sauce
6 g sesame oil

Garnishing
4 tsp fried shallots
4 tsp chopped spring onion
1 large red chilli, sliced

NUTRITION INFORMATION

	Per Serve (109.2g)	Per 100 g
Energy (kcal)	266	243
Protein (g)	8.0	7.4
Total fat (g)	9.3	8.5
Saturated fat (g)	0.9	0.8
Trans fat (g)	0	0
Cholesterol (mg)	8	7.3
Carbohydrate (g)	35.4	32.4
Dietary fibre (g)	3.2	2.9
Sodium (mg)	263	241

Method

1. Soak dried mushrooms and dried shrimps together until softened.
2. Drain mushrooms and shrimps and set aside. Measure soaking liquid and top up with more water to make 600 ml.
3. Dice mushrooms. Mince shrimps and shallots. Place in a bowl.
4. Peel pumpkin and yam and cut into cubes. Place in another bowl.
5. In a mixing bowl, combine rice flour and tapioca starch. Add soaking liquid and whisk until there are no lumps. Set aside.
6. Bring a pot of water to the boil and cook pumpkin and yam for about 5 minutes until just done. Remove from heat and set aside.
7. Heat a wok over medium heat. Add oil and stir-fry mushrooms, shrimps and shallots for about 2 minutes until fragrant.
8. Add pre-cooked pumpkin and yam and stir-fry for about 1 minute.
9. Add seasoning and stir-fry for another minute.

Tip: To enhance the taste of this dish, use the soaking liquid from the dried shrimps and mushrooms to make the batter. If there is insufficient soaking liquid, simply top up with water.

(Recipe continues)

10. Lower the heat and add rice flour mixture.
11. As mixture continues to cook, it will start to become sticky. Stir continuously until mixture comes together, but is still able to fall off a spoon easily. (See photos for consistency.) The mixture has to be cooked just right. Undercook it and it will not form a cake when steamed. Overcook it and the texture will be rubbery and tough after steaming.

Just nice   Overcooked   Undercooked

12. Oil a baking tray with 1 tsp oil. Pour mixture into tray and level it.
13. Place baking tray in steamer and steam for 1 hour. Test for doneness by inserting a wooden skewer into the centre of yam cake. It should come out clean. Continue steaming if needed.
14. Remove yam cake from steamer and set aside to cool.
15. Unmould yam cake from baking tray.
16. Slice and garnish with fried shallots, spring onion and sliced chilli before serving.

Yoghurt Tiramisu

SERVES 3

Although this isn't an Asian dish, we couldn't resist sharing it as it is a favourite dessert among many. What's more, our version is lower in saturated fat and calories, being layered with creamy and slightly tangy Greek yoghurt. Who can blame us?

Ingredients

Yoghurt Mixture (4 servings)
200 g Greek yoghurt
174 g plain regular yoghurt
40 g icing sugar
1¼ tsp vanilla essence
1¼ tbsp cocoa powder

Lady Finger Biscuit Layer
2½ tsp instant coffee powder
2½ tbsp hot water
12–14 lady finger biscuits

Method

Preparing the Yoghurt Mixture
1. In a bowl, combine Greek yoghurt, regular yoghurt, icing sugar and vanilla essence. Mix well and pass mixture through a sieve to remove any lumps.

Preparing the Lady Finger Biscuit Layer
2. In another bowl, combine instant coffee powder with hot water. Mix to dissolve. (Note: Use more water if you prefer a lighter coffee flavour.)
3. Place 6–7 lady finger biscuits in a small baking tray/bowl. Drizzle with half the coffee mixture.
4. Top lady finger biscuits with half the prepared yoghurt mixture.
5. Top with another layer of lady finger biscuits. Drizzle with remaining coffee mixture and cover with remaining yoghurt mixture.
6. Dust with cocoa powder.
7. Cover and refrigerate for at least 30 minutes before serving.

NUTRITION INFORMATION

	Per Serve (159 g)	Per 100 g
Energy (kcal)	303	190
Protein (g)	10.0	6.3
Total fat (g)	3.0	1.9
Saturated fat (g)	1.0	0.6
Trans fat (g)	0	0
Cholesterol (mg)	48	30
Carbohydrate (g)	55.7	35
Dietary fibre (g)	3.6	2.3
Sodium (mg)	170	107

Tip: For an even tastier treat, store the tiramisu in the fridge overnight before serving. The sitting time will allow the flavours to meld and develop.

Weights & Measures

Quantities for this book are given in metric and American (spoon) measures. Standard spoon measurements used are: 1 teaspoon = 5 ml and 1 tablespoon = 15 ml. All measures are level unless otherwise stated.

LIQUID AND VOLUME MEASURES

Metric	Imperial	American
5 ml	$1/6$ fl oz	1 teaspoon
10 ml	$1/3$ fl oz	1 dessertspoon
15 ml	$1/2$ fl oz	1 tablespoon
60 ml	2 fl oz	$1/4$ cup (4 tablespoons)
85 ml	$2^{1}/_{2}$ fl oz	$1/3$ cup
90 ml	3 fl oz	$3/8$ cup (6 tablespoons)
125 ml	4 fl oz	$1/2$ cup
180 ml	6 fl oz	$3/4$ cup
250 ml	8 fl oz	1 cup
300 ml	10 fl oz ($1/2$ pint)	$1^{1}/_{4}$ cups
375 ml	12 fl oz	$1^{1}/_{2}$ cups
435 ml	14 fl oz	$1^{3}/_{4}$ cups
500 ml	16 fl oz	2 cups
625 ml	20 fl oz (1 pint)	$2^{1}/_{2}$ cups
750 ml	24 fl oz ($1^{1}/_{5}$ pints)	3 cups
1 litre	32 fl oz ($1^{3}/_{5}$ pints)	4 cups
1.25 litres	40 fl oz (2 pints)	5 cups
1.5 litres	48 fl oz ($2^{2}/_{5}$ pints)	6 cups
2.5 litres	80 fl oz (4 pints)	10 cups

OVEN TEMPERATURE

	°C	°F	Gas Regulo
Very slow	120	250	1
Slow	150	300	2
Moderately slow	160	325	3
Moderate	180	350	4
Moderately hot	190/200	370/400	5/6
Hot	210/220	410/440	6/7
Very hot	230	450	8
Super hot	250/290	475/550	9/10

DRY MEASURES

Metric	Imperial
30 grams	1 ounce
45 grams	$1^{1}/_{2}$ ounces
55 grams	2 ounces
70 grams	$2^{1}/_{2}$ ounces
85 grams	3 ounces
100 grams	$3^{1}/_{2}$ ounces
110 grams	4 ounces
125 grams	$4^{1}/_{2}$ ounces
140 grams	5 ounces
280 grams	10 ounces
450 grams	16 ounces (1 pound)
500 grams	1 pound, $1^{1}/_{2}$ ounces
700 grams	$1^{1}/_{2}$ pounds
800 grams	$1^{3}/_{4}$ pounds
1 kilogram	2 pounds, 3 ounces
1.5 kilograms	3 pounds, $4^{1}/_{2}$ ounces
2 kilograms	4 pounds, 6 ounces

LENGTH

Metric	Imperial
0.5 cm	$1/4$ inch
1 cm	$1/2$ inch
1.5 cm	$3/4$ inch
2.5 cm	1 inch

ABBREVIATION

tsp	teaspoon
tbsp	tablespoon
g	gram
kg	kilogram
ml	millilitre